To all the teachers I've had throughout my life,
I love and thank you all—

You all shaped me, taught me,
and maybe even annoyed me,
and you definitely made me think.
For that, I am forever grateful. ❤️

Thank you 🩷

Aarav has the most annoying teacher ever.
Mrs. O'Hare always gives out homework every single night, even on Fridays!
"Give us a break!" whines Aarav.

Mrs. O'Hare is **so** annoying!

BUT...

deep inside, Aarav knows that doing the homework helps him understand things better and makes him feel smart in class.

Mi Young has the most annoying teacher ever.
Mr. DeSantis always calls on her to answer questions, even when she doesn't raise her hand.

Mr. DeSantis is **so** annoying!

BUT...

deep inside, Mi Young knows that Mr. DeSantis believes in her and wants her to be confident in what she knows.

Juan Marcos has the most annoying teacher ever.
Ms. Calderwood never lets the class have extra recess, no matter how much they ask.

Ms. Calderwood is **so** annoying!

BUT...

deep inside, Juan Marcos knows that Ms. Calderwood just wants them to learn as much as possible and recess will come soon enough.

Sophia has the most annoying teacher ever.
Mr. Patel always checks their desks for neatness and makes them clean up every day.

Mr. Patel is **so** annoying!

BUT...

deep inside, Sophia knows that keeping her space clean and tidy helps her stay organized and focused.

Mila has the most annoying teacher ever.
Ms. Garrie can never figure out how to work the projector.
"Can't you just press the button?" Mila mutters.

Ms. Garrie is **SO** annoying!

BUT...

deep inside, Mila knows Ms. Garrie is trying her best, and when the lesson finally starts, it's always worth the wait.

Mr. Fuamatu talks so loudly, the whole school can hear him.
"Why are you yelling?" Grace wonders.

Mr. Fuamatu is **SO** annoying!

BUT...

deep inside, Grace knows Mr. Fuamatu just wants to make sure everyone pays attention and hears what's important.

Olivia has the most annoying teacher ever.
Ms. Carter makes them walk in a perfectly straight line everywhere they go.

Ms. Carter is **so** annoying!

BUT...

deep inside, Olivia knows that Ms. Carter is teaching them how to be responsible and respectful in school.

Congratulations, Olivia!

Citizenship Award

Jack has the most annoying teacher ever.

Ms. Grayson follows every single rule in the handbook, even the silly ones.

"We seriously can't wear red on Tuesdays?" Jack groans.

Ms. Grayson is **SO** annoying!

BUT...

deep inside, Jack knows Ms. Grayson just wants to be fair and make sure everyone knows how to follow the rules.

No Red on Tuesdays

Beto has the most annoying teacher ever.
Mr. Rivers always talks about history, even when no one asks.

Mr. Rivers is **so** annoying!

BUT...

deep inside, Beto knows that Mr. Rivers loves history and wants them to see how exciting the past can be.

Shonda has the most annoying teacher ever.
Ms. Eriksson never lets the class turn in late assignments, no matter the excuse.
"Can't you cut us some slack?" Shonda groans.

Ms. Eriksson is **SO** annoying!

BUT...

deep inside, Shonda knows Ms. Eriksson just wants them to be responsible and ready for the future.

Future Leaders of America

Lila has the most annoying teacher ever.

Mrs. Kowalski starts a lesson, but somehow ends up telling stories about her pet pot-bellied pig.

"Can we just stick to the topic?" Lila complains.

Mrs. Kowalski is **SO** annoying!

BUT...

deep inside, Lila knows Mrs. Kowalski's stories make the class laugh and keep the lessons interesting, even if they take a little longer.

Sy has the most annoying teacher ever.
Mr. García always calls on Zoe first and gives her extra compliments.
"Why can't we all get some recognition?" Sy protests.

Mr. García is **SO** annoying!

BUT...

deep inside, Zy knows Mr. García believes in everyone and just shows it differently sometimes.

Maira has the most annoying teacher ever.
Ms. Sutton always forgets her name and calls her "Mary" instead.
"Can't you remember just once?" Maira sighs.

Ms. Sutton is **SO** annoying!

BUT...

deep inside, Maira knows Ms. Sutton is trying her best and cares about all her students, even if she gets a little mixed up.

Noah has the most annoying teacher ever.
Mr. Svoboda spends 20 minutes explaining how to sharpen a pencil.
"We got it the first time!" Noah groans.

Mr. Svoboda is **SO** annoying!

BUT...

deep inside, Noah knows Mr. Svoboda just wants to make sure no one is left behind and everyone feels confident.

Tyler has the most annoying teacher ever.
Ms. Howard plays cheerful music during quiet work time.
"Can't we just have silence?" Tyler wishes.

Ms. Howard is **SO** annoying!

BUT...

deep inside, Tyler knows Ms. Howard just wants them to feel relaxed and enjoy learning.

Marquita has the most annoying teacher ever.
Mrs. Wilson always gives surprise quizzes when they least expect it.
"Why can't you warn us?" Marquita grumbles.

Mrs. Wilson is **SO** annoying!

BUT...

deep inside, Marquita knows Mrs. Wilson just wants to make sure they're really learning and ready for anything.

Max has the most annoying teacher ever.
Mr. Thomas always makes them redo their group projects, if they didn't work well together.
"Can't we just turn this thing in?" Max objects.

Mr. Thomas is **SO** annoying!

BUT...

deep inside, Max knows Mr. Thomas wants them to learn how to cooperate and be a great team.

Do you have the most annoying teacher ever?
Well, you might.

BUT...

deep inside, what you probably also know is that the most annoying teachers are the ones who care the most about helping you succeed and grow.

Thank **your favorite** teacher:

_____

_____

_____

_____

_____

_____

_____

www.ingramcontent.com/pod-product-compliance
Lightning Source LLC
LaVergne TN
LVHW072055070426
835508LV00002B/100